Published simultaneously in 1994 by Exley Publications
in Great Britain, and Exley Giftbooks in the USA.
**Selection and arrangement © Helen Exley 1994**
**ISBN 1-85015-449-X**

Edited by Helen Exley.
Text researched by Margaret Montgomery.
Designed by Pinpoint Design.
Picture research P. A. Goldberg & J. M. Clift/Image Select.
Typeset by Delta, Watford.
Printed and bound by William Clowes, Beccles.
Exley Publications Ltd, 16 Chalk Hill, Watford, Herts WD1 4BN, U.K.
Exley Giftbooks, 232 Madison Avenue, Suite 1206, New York,
NY 10016, USA.
Exley Publications is very grateful to the following individuals and organizations for
permission to reproduce their pictures: Archiv Für Kunst (AKG), Art Resource (AR),
The Bridgeman Art Library (BAL), Fine Art Photographic Library (FAP). Special
thanks to Hilary Burn, Peter Kettle and Andrew Stock for their assistance in
providing illustrations. Cover: © 1994 Hilary Burn "Heron" (detail); page 5 (Title
page): © 1994 Hilary Burn "Little Owl" (detail); page 6: (AKG) Egyptian wallpainting,
12th dynasty; page 11: (BAL) © 1994 Julian Novorol, "Pinkfeet out of Loch Leven,
Fife", private collection; page 12: (FAP) A. E. Bailey, by courtesy of David Messum
Gallery, Beaconsfield; page 14: © 1994 Andrew Stock, "Goldfinches" (detail); page 17:
(BAL) Joseph Crawhall, The Fine Art Society, London; page 19: © 1994 Peter Kettle
"A Sparrow at Lambeth"; page 21: (FAP) Archibald Thorburn; page 23: © 1994 Hilary
Burn, "Wrens" (detail); page 25: © 1994 Hilary Burn "Buzzard" (detail); page 27:
(AKG) Zoological plate of falcon; page 28: © 1994, Peter Kettle, "Heron at Clifton";
page 31: (BAL) Koson, private collection; page 32: © 1994 Andrew Stock, "Young
Bluetit"; page 34: © 1994 Andrew Stock, "Puffins" (detail); page 36: (BAL) John James
Audubon, Victoria & Albert Museum, London; page 38: (BAL) © 1994 Douglas
Anderson, "Seagulls in Bog" (detail), Ackermann and Johnson Ltd., London; page 41:
(BAL) David Adolph Constant Artz, Gavin Graham Gallery, London; page 43: © 1994
Hilary Burn "Dipper"; page 44: © 1994 Hilary Burn "Marsh Tit"; page 47: (AKG)
Claude Monet, Musée d'Orsay, Paris; page 48: © Hilary Burn "Female Goosander and
Chicks"; page 51: (AKG) Adolph von Menzel, Nationalgalerie, Berlin; page 52: (AKG)
Adolph von Menzel; Page 55: © 1994 Michael Loates "Reed Bunting", Malcolm
Innes Gallery, London; page 57: (FAP) John James Audubon, courtesy Beaton Brown
Fine Paintings, London SW1; page 59: (AR) John James Audubon, Howard Jensen/
Scala; page 61: (BAL) © 1994 Julian Novorol "Teal Seek Shelter" (detail), private
collection; page 63: (BAL) John James Audubon, Victoria & Albert Museum, London.

# BIRDS

## A CELEBRATION
## IN WORDS
## AND PAINTINGS

SELECTED BY
HELEN EXLEY

**EXLEY**
NEW YORK · WATFORD, UK

Sweet is the breath of morn, her rising sweet
with charm of earliest birds.

**JOHN MILTON (1608-1674)**

෴

I was reminded, this morning before I rose, of
those undescribed ambrosial mornings of
summer which I can remember, when a
thousand birds were heard gently twittering
and ushering in the light, like the argument to a
new canto of an epic and heroic poem. The
serenity, the infinite promise, of such a
morning! The song or twitter of birds drips from
the leaves like dew. Then there was something
divine and immortal in our life, when I have
wakened up on my couch in the woods and seen
the day dawning, and heard the twittering of
the birds.

**HENRY DAVID THOREAU (1817-1862)**

෴

Hear how the birds, on ev'ry blooming spray,
With joyous musick wake the dawning day!

**ALEXANDER POPE (1688-1744)**

෴

# SPRING SONG

Listening to that insistent sound I was reminded of Warde Fowler's words about the sweet season which brings new life and hope to men, and how a seal and sanction is put on it by that same small bird's clear resonant voice....

**W. H. HUDSON (1841-1922)**

As a rule the wonderful notes are uttered on the wing, and are the accompaniment of a graceful flight that has motions of evident pleasure. The notes do not sound passionate: they suggest peace, rest, healing, joy, an assurance of happiness past, present and to come. To listen to curlews on a bright, clear April day, with the fullness of spring still in anticipation, is one of the best experiences that a lover of birds can have.

**VISCOUNT GREY OF FALLODON,**
**FROM *"THE CHARM OF BIRDS"***

One swallow does not make a summer, but one skein of geese, cleaving the murk of a March thaw, is the Spring.

**ALDO LEOPOLD (1886-1948)**

For me there are few more enjoyable experiences than seeing my first swallow of the year, even if it is only a brief flash of deep metallic blue and an impression of grace and beauty as the bird flies low on its way to its summer home....

**PETER TATE,**
**FROM** *"SWALLOWS"*

Here's summer. The swallows have brought it, wheeling above the town, greeting familiar roofs and rivulets – all as they remembered.

Stay long, my friends – for summer will end as you set out again.

**JESSE O'NEILL**

Surely, I said, this spring-time verdure and bloom, this fragrance of the furze, the infinite blue of heaven, the bell-like double note of this my little feathered neighbour in the alder tree, slitting hither and thither, light and airy himself as a wind-fluttered alder leaf – surely this is enough to fill and to satisfy any heart, leaving no room for a grief so vain and barren, which nothing in nature suggested!

**W. H. HUDSON (1841-1922)**

I sat on a hillside in the woods late in the day amid the pines and hemlocks, and heard the soft, elusive spring call of the little owl – a curious musical undertone hardly separable from the silence; a bell, muffled in feathers tolling in the twilight of the woods and discernible only to the most alert ear. But it was the voice of spring.

JOHN BURROUGHS,
FROM *"RIVERBY"*

And after April, when May follows,
And the whitethroat builds, and all the
swallows –
Hark! where my blossomed pear-tree in the hedge
Leans to the field and scatters on the clover
Blossoms and dewdrops – at the bent-spray's
edge –
That's the wise thrush; he sings each song twice
over
Lest you should think he never could recapture
The first fine careless rapture!

ROBERT BROWNING (1812-1889),
FROM *"HOME THOUGHTS, FROM ABROAD"*

# SPRING-TIME

Imagine yourself in a green dell, where the meadows meet the wood, a soft warm wind gently blowing, and the big white clouds above sailing under a dome of blue.

All around you, in the bushes, in the trees, and up in the sky, there is music: Thrushes and Blackbirds whistling their pure notes from the bushes; Linnets flitting on the yellow gorse, singing their softer liquid songs; Cuckoos calling in the fields; Warblers singing in the wood, and Larks soaring over all. Flowers everywhere, butterflies dancing over them, and the air itself filled with the more faint music of insects' wings. Wherever you look there is happiness, for the whole world is awake and mad with a great joy.

OLIVER G. PIKE,
FROM *"BIRDLAND"*

I wish you the happiness of birds
Hawk hover. Skylark's song
Nightingales –
A spurt of silver sound in the tangled wood
Starlings –
A swirl of smoke against the evening sky
Robin on the spade.
Blackbird on the chimney pot.
A heron flapping home.
And wild geese calling as they pass
– a sudden rush of wings above our lifted heads.
Rooks tumbling down the wind
And mousy wrens running along the hedge foot
Swans
A dazzle of finches
A drift of night owls
An impudence of starlings.

Companions light as air
Fragile as flowers
yet bold, bright, vividly aware
Lives like our own.

**PAM BROWN, b.1928**

I am happy because the birds sing to me.

JOSEPHINE, aged 6,
FROM *"A CHILD'S VIEW OF HAPPINESS"*

I hope you love birds too.
It is economical.
It saves going to Heaven.

EMILY DICKINSON (1830-1886),
FROM *"LETTERS OF EMILY DICKINSON"*

# FRIENDS

I once had a sparrow alight upon my shoulder,
while hoeing in a village garden, and I felt I
was more distinguished by that circumstance
than I should have been by any epaulet I could
have worn.

**HENRY DAVID THOREAU (1817-1862)**

A garden full of spuggies (known to polite
people as house sparrows) might not
appeal to everyone, but for endless fun and
chatter it's hard to beat. All birds provide
moments of joy. Spuggies provide continual
companionship.

**TEEARE SCARROTT,
FROM *"BIRDS MAGAZINE"***

How great the reverence I feel when a small
bird accepts me as a friend.

**HELEN THOMSON, b.1943**

I never saw a wild thing sorry for itself.

**D. H. LAWRENCE (1885-1930)**

How, in the extreme terrors of its existence, can a bird sing so happily? There is no hint of fear in the song of any bird, nor does terror mar the beauty of its life. It seems able to live entirely in the moment, isolating its joys and fears.

**CLARE LEIGHTON,
FROM *"FOUR HEDGES"***

[Birds] also use flight to express blissful well-being; by this as well as by song they are gifted beyond all other creatures to convey to the mind of man the existence of happiness and joy.

**VISCOUNT GREY OF FALLODON**

The joy of life.... The sense of living – the consciousness of seeing and feeling – is manifestly intense in them all, and is in itself an exquisite pleasure.

**RICHARD JEFFERIES (1848-1887)**

W<sub>ren</sub>
Neat as a nut, perk-tailed and needle-beaked,
your stripings drawn with the finest brush, your
eyes aware, you scuttle through the fallen
leaves like a little mouse. So small. So very
small.

And yet your song fills the garden – defying
any other wren in ear shot. Shrill, clear – a
reed-thin trumpet call.

CHARLOTTE GRAY, b.1937

∕∽∽

..."energy" is the wren's middle name, and his
dynamic presence in the garden is sometimes an
uncomfortable spur to the would-be lazy
individual who prefers sun-bathing to work!

ANNE BLAKEMORE,
FROM "WHO SIT AND WATCH"

∕∽∽

B<sub>irds</sub> please because they are so visibly and so
audibly, such willing partners in life. Their
vitality is infectious.

FROM "THE TIMES"

∕∽∽

# FLYING FREE

Birds, the free tenants of land, air, and ocean,
Their forms all symmetry, their motions
  grace....

**JAMES MONTGOMERY (1771-1864)**

The wild goose comes north with the voice
of freedom and adventure. He is more
than a big, far-ranging bird; he is the
epitome of wanderlust, limitless
horizons and distant travel. He is the
yearning and the dream, the search and
the wonder, the unfettered foot and the
wind's-will wing.

**HAL BORLAND (1900-1978)**

The bluebird carries the sky on his back.

**HENRY DAVID THOREAU (1817-1862)**

The birds – are they worth remembering?
Is flight a wonder and one wingtip a space
    marvel?
When will man know what birds know?

CARL SANDBURG (1878-1967),
FROM *"WINGTIP"*

I caught this morning morning's minion,
    kingdom of daylight's dauphin, dapple-dawn-
    drawn Falcon, in his riding
    Of the rolling level underneath him steady
        air, and striding
High there, how he rung upon the rein of a
wimpling wing
In his ecstasy! then off, off forth on swing,
    As a skate's heel sweeps smooth on a bow-
        bend: the hurl and gliding
    Rebuffed the big wind. My heart in hiding
Stirred for a bird, – the achieve of, the mastery
    of the thing!

GERARD MANLEY HOPKINS, (1844-1899),
FROM *"THE WINDHOVER"*

Learning the secret of flight from a bird was a good deal like learning the secret of magic from a magician.

ORVILLE WRIGHT (1871-1948)

I think more of a bird with broad wings flying
and lapsing through the air, than anything,
when I think of metre.

**D. H. LAWRENCE (1885-1930)**

One of the sights that never grows stale, flat,
or unprofitable is the flight of a bird: the slow
sail of the gull, the muscular dash of a pigeon,
the smooth speed of the swallow's circles, the
wayward patrol of the peewit, the sudden
twists and swerves of turtle dove or of golden
plover, the hover and stoop of the kestrel, the
fountain-like dance of the grey wagtail or
flycatcher, the massed manoeuvres of starlings,
the slow beat of the heron that can yet climb
in rivalry with the peregrine, the purposeful
spearhead of migrating duck or geese, the
spiral of the lark, the sharply angled ascent
and fall of the tree pipit – all flight is a
luxury to the beholder.

**SIR WILLIAM BEACH THOMAS**

It was the Rainbow gave thee birth,
And left thee all her lovely hues.

**W. H. DAVIES (1871-1940),**
**FROM "THE KINGFISHER"**

Remember that the most beautiful things in the world are the most useless; peacocks and lilies for instance.

**JOHN RUSKIN (1819-1900)**

Have you ever observed a humming-bird moving about in an aerial dance among the flowers – a living prismatic gem that changes with every change of position – how in turning it catches the sunshine on its burnished neck and gorget plumes – green and gold and flame-coloured, the beams changing to visible flakes as they fall, dissolving into nothing, to be succeeded by others and yet others? In its exquisite form...its swift motions and intervals of aerial suspension, it is a creature of such fairy-like loveliness as to mock all description.

**W. H. HUDSON (1841-1922)**

A bird's life is so frail, so threatened, that each is a miracle – each new hatching an astonishment.

HELEN THOMSON, b.1943

To be a bird is to be alive more intensively than any other living creature.... [Birds] live in a world that is always the present, mostly full of joy.

N. J. BERRILL

To hold a living bird in one's hands is to be changed.

Before that moment these creatures were simply a decoration, an element in the background to our own existence.

But now they are transformed to individuals, hearts pounding, eyes searching, throats calling as they live out lives as vital as our own.

JANE SWAN, b.1943

# LIVES OF WONDER

Adventurers from space would return to
their planet with no reports of our technology,
our skyscrapers. They would tell of the
green, the living green and of the birds,
the soaring, sweeping, singing multitude
that live their lives of wonder, free from our
small human concerns.

**HELEN THOMSON, b.1943**

Do you ne'er think what wondrous
   beings these?
Do you ne'er think who made them,
   and who taught
The dialect they speak, where melodies
Alone are the interpreters of thought?

**HENRY WADSWORTH LONGFELLOW (1807-1882)**

I cannot adequately explain the fascination
which the wild birds have for me, and, in these
days, for an increasing multitude of people.
Is it their flight, so mysterious even yet to us,
their grace and beauty, their fulness of
abounding life, the interest of their nesting,
the charm of their varied surroundings,
the exhilaration of the quest which lures
us forth into the open? It is all these
and more, and fortunate are they who feel
the thrill of enthusiasm for nature and
in nature, be the special interest birds or
whatsoever it may.

**HERBERT K. JOB,
FROM *"WILD WINGS"***

Ivory-billed Woodpecker Male 1.2 & Female 3.
PICUS PRINCIPALIS.

My childhood was full of birdsong – the deafening clamour of the dawn chorus – the sweet, bright song of larks descending – the chattering of sparrows in the eves – the scream of swifts scything between the houses – the evening blackbird singing his last, late song from the chimney pot.

I am not so very old. And yet – where have they gone?

Will my grandchild, waking early, open her window, lean out into the cool air of the dawn and hear the waterfall of song that I once knew?

PAM BROWN, b.1928

...birds are far more than robins, thrushes, and finches to brighten the suburban garden, or ducks and grouse to fill the sportsman's bag, or rare waders or warblers to be ticked off on a bird watcher's checklist. They are indicators of the environment – a sort of environmental litmus-paper.

ROGER TORY PETERSON, b.1908

When you have shot one bird flying you have shot all birds flying.

**ERNEST HEMINGWAY (1899-1961)**

Shoot all the bluejays you want, if you can hit 'em, but remember it's a sin to kill a mockingbird.... Mockingbirds don't do one thing but make music for us to enjoy. They don't eat up people's gardens, don't nest in corncribs, they don't do one thing but sing their hearts out for us. That's why it's a sin to kill a mockingbird.

**HARPER LEE, b.1926,**
**FROM *"TO KILL A MOCKINGBIRD"***

It lay on the shore. Among the stones. A lifeless, black heap. It had no soft downy plumage any more, it is sticky, oily, forbidding. It died because of man.
"Well, it is only a seagull. Or a tern. They are so common."

**HANNA SAARINEN, aged 13**

How good to be a duck.
To float lightly on the water, the ripples
    touching one's feathers like gentle fingers.
To nonchalantly upend and dabble in the
    flickering shadows of the weed.
To proudly lead a bobbing of ducklings and call
    the stragglers home at a skittering rush.
To drowse beneath willows in gentle company
To launch into the air and leave water and tree
    and grass far, far below – the sounds of earth
    falling away, lost in the hush of wings.

PAM BROWN, b.1928

⌒

Being suspicious of us, she [the dabchick] had
warned the young and now presented her body
to them as they sat in the water. Instinct told
them what was required: each bird got on to the
back of the old one, and was there covered by
her folded wings. When all the young had
mounted, the parent swam away with her whole
family, compact, concealed and safe.

VISCOUNT GREY OF FALLODON

⌒

# SOLITARY SONG

It was only a bird call at evening, unidentified,
As I came from the spring with water, across
   the rocky back-pasture;
But so still I stood sky above was not stiller
   the sky in pail-water.

⸺ •• ••• ⸺

Years pass, all places and faces fade, some
   people have died,
And I stand in a far land, the evening still, and
   am at last sure
That I miss more that stillness at bird-call than
   some things that were to fail later.

**ROBERT PENN WARREN (1905-1989),
FROM** *"ORNITHOLOGY IN A WORLD OF FLUX"*

Solitary the thrush,
The hermit withdrawn to himself, avoiding the
settlements,
Sings by himself a song.

**WALT WHITMAN (1819-1892)**

Magic birds were dancing in the mystic marsh. The grass swayed with them, and the shallow waters, and the earth fluttered under them. The earth was dancing with the cranes, and the low sun, and the wind and sky.

MARJORIE KINNAN RAWLINGS (1896-1953)

⤫

Early summer days are a jubilee time for birds. In the fields around the house, in the barn, in the woods, in the swamp – everywhere love and songs and nests and eggs. From the edge of the woods, the white-throated sparrow (which must come all the way from Boston) calls, "Oh, Peabody, Peabody, Peabody!" On an apple bough, the phoebe teeters and wags its tail and says, "Phoebe, phoe-bee!" The song sparrow, who knows how brief and lovely life is, says, "Sweet, sweet, sweet interlude; sweet, sweet, sweet interlude." If you enter the barn, the swallows swoop down from their nests and scold. "Cheeky, cheeky!" they say.

E. B. WHITE (1899-1985),
FROM *"CHARLOTTE'S WEB"*

⤫

Humans have persuaded themselves that God gave them birds to be of use – as flesh and feather, as objects of rare beauty, as voices to enchant. And as we have caged them, plucked them, roasted them, we have still claimed that in life they sang to praise a mutual creator.

A thrush sings simply for another thrush.
She is not grateful if we do not shoot her.
It is we who should be grateful.

**JANE SWAN, b.1943**

❧

We do not need this little bird as much as we need the qualities required to spare its life.

**DEIRDRE PLATT, aged 16**

❧

I saw with open eyes
Singing birds sweet
Sold in the shops
For the people to eat,
Sold in the shops of
Stupidity Street.

**RALPH HODGSON (1871-1962)**

❧

I suppose this is why so many people feel a sense of affinity with birds. Our admiration for their bright colors, sweet songs, and graceful flight suggests that some very large part of our brains is still up in the canopy with them....

**DAVID RAINES WALLACE**

One touch of nature makes the whole world kin.

**WILLIAM SHAKESPEARE (1564-1616)**

[The nightingale's song] is only a bird song, yet is undeniably musical and expressive, and seems to involve something close to aesthetic choice on the part of the bird. And in touching us emotionally it begins to stray over that crucial line by which we separate ourselves (and our supposedly unique gifts) from the rest of creation.

RICHARD MABEY,
FROM *"WHISTLING IN THE DARK"*

Although birds coexist with us on this eroded planet, they live independently of us with a self-sufficiency that is almost a rebuke. In the world of birds a symposium on the purpose of life would be inconceivable. They do not need it. We are not that self reliant. We are the ones who have lost our way.

BROOKS ATKINSON (1894-1984)

Sit outside at midnight and close your eyes; feel the grass, the air, the space. Listen to birds for ten minutes at dawn. Memorize a flower.

LINDA HASSELSTROM

Nature, in her blind search for life, has filled every possible cranny of the earth with some sort of fantastic creature.

**JOSEPH WOOD KRUTCH**

⁓⁓

I like the ridiculous birds. The stork with a nose like a shovel and enormous knees. The owl spinning its head like something from a horror movie. Ducks ashore. Ostriches. I like the workaday birds. Sparrows and starlings, hens.

I like the magical birds. Geese stretched like a skein of silk across the evening sky and calling loons. I like the amazing birds. Hoopoes and avocets. Humming birds. Bee eaters.

I like the birds that rule the sky. Eagles and larks. Swifts and swallows. Gulls.

Like? Love. Need. Rejoice in.

**PAM BROWN, b.1928**

⁓⁓

There are no grotesques in nature.

**THOMAS BROWNE**

⁓⁓

# LEARNING FROM THE BIRDS

Let a thousand men set up their houses in a wood, and the wood becomes a hideous small town. Let a thousand birds settle in the same wood, and it will take a skilled eye to find even twenty of them.

ROBERT LYND (1879-1949),
FROM *"THE BLUE LION"*

Ye children of Man, whose life is a span
Protracted with sorrow from day to day,
Naked and featherless, feeble and querulous,
Sickly calamitous creatures of clay;
Attend to the words of the sovereign birds,
Immortal illustrious lords of the air,
Who survey from on high with a merciful eye
Your struggles of misery, labour and care.
Whence you may learn and clearly discern
Such truths as attract your inquisitive turn.

ARISTOPHANES (c.448-c.388 B.C.),
FROM *"THE BIRDS"*

As I come over the hill, I hear the wood thrush singing his evening lay. This is the only bird whose note affects me like music, affects the flow and tenor of my thoughts, my fancy and imagination. It lifts and exhilarates.... It is a medicative draught to my soul. It is an elixir to my eyes and a fountain of youth to all my senses. It changes all hours to an eternal morning. It banishes all trivialness. It reinstates me in my dominion, makes me the lord of creation, is chief musician of my court.

**HENRY DAVID THOREAU (1817-1862)**

The voice I hear this passing night was heard
  In ancient days by emperor and clown:
Perhaps the self-same song that found a path
  Through the sad heart of Ruth, when, sick for home,
    She stood in tears amid the alien corn;
      The same that oft-times hath
Charm'd magic casements, opening on the foam
  Of perilous seas, in faery lands forlorn.

**JOHN KEATS (1795-1821),**
**FROM** *"ODE TO A NIGHTINGALE"*

# A SONG THROUGH MY LIFE

...to listen to stars and birds, to babes and sages, with open heart.... This is to be my symphony.

**WILLIAM HENRY CHANNING (1810-1884)**

I wake to the chattering of sparrows under the eaves, to sunlight dappling the curtains, to a new day.
   And for a moment I am out of time –
the birds seem the same that woke me
as a child.
   And the waiting day promises the same joy.

**HELEN THOMSON, b.1943**

Bury me where the birds will sing
over my grave.

**ALEXANDER WILSON (1766-1813)**

# ...THE VAST WILDERNESS

The loons of Lac la Croix are part of the vast
solitudes, the hundreds of rocky islands, the
long reaches of the lake toward the Maligne, the
Snake, and the Namakon. My memory is full of
their calling: in the morning when the white
horses of the mists are galloping out of the bays,
at midday when their long, lazy bugling is part
of the calm, and at dusk when their music joins
with that of the hermit thrushes and the
wilderness is going to sleep.

SIGURD F. OLSON

The sun, as it rose, tinged the quicksilver of the
creeks.... The curlew, who had been piping their
mournful plaints since long before the light,
flew now from weed-bank to weed-bank.... The
black-guard of crows rose from the pine trees on
the dunes with merry cheers. Shore birds of
every sort populated the tide line, filling it with
business and beauty.

T. H. WHITE (1906-1964)

Did you ever chance to hear the midnight flight of birds passing through the air and darkness overhead, in countless armies, changing their early, or late summer habitat? It is something not to be forgotten....

**WALT WHITMAN (1819-1892)**

The little flock [of sanderlings] wheeled out over the bay in a wide circle, flashing white wing bars; they returned, crying loudly as they passed over the flats where the young were still running and probing at the edge of the curling wavelets; they turned their heads to the south and were gone.

**RACHEL CARSON (1907-1964)**

The swallows are gathering. Gossiping along the wires. Flickering in their restlessness. And suddenly are gone. And summer with them.

**JENNY DE VRIES (1947-1991)**